A Whale Biologist at Work

Sneed B. Collard III

A Wildlife Conservation Society Book

Franklin Watts
A Division of Grolier Publishing
New York • London • Hong Kong • Sydney
Danbury, Connecticut

*For Scott Callow, my great friend
and longtime biology buddy*

Visit Franklin Watts on the Internet at
http://publishing.grolier.com

Library of Congress Cataloging-in-Publication Data

Collard, Sneed B.
A whale biologist at work / by Sneed B. Collard III.
        p. cm.– (Wildlife conservation society books)
        Includes bibliographical references and index.
        Summary: Describes the work of marine biologist John Calambokidis, who studies whales off the coast of California.
        ISBN 0-531-11786-3 (lib. bdg.)   0-531-16521-4 (pbk.)
        1. Calambokidis, John, 1954–Juvenile literature. [1. Chipmunks.] 2. Marine biologists—United States Biography Juvenile literature. 3. Humpback whale Juvenile literature. 4. Blue whale Juvenile literature. [1. Marine biologists. 2. Occupations. 3. Whales. 4. Calambokidis, John, 1954– .] I. Title. II. Series.
QL31.C15C65   2000
578.77'092–dc21   99-40941
[B]   CIP

©2000 Sneed B. Collard III
All rights reserved. Published simultaneously in Canada.
Printed in the United States of America.
1 2 3 4 5 6 7 8 9 10 R 09 08 07 06 05 04 03 02 01 00

GROLIER
PUBLISHING

Contents

Meet the Author

Author Sneed B. Collard III on a whale watch

Sneed B. Collard III is the author of more than twenty award-winning science and nature books for young people. Each year, Mr. Collard travels widely, speaking to thousands of students and teachers throughout the United States. He lives in Missoula, Montana.

"For many years, people in southern California have enjoyed going out in boats to watch gray whales migrate up and down the Pacific coast. In the summer of 1992, however, people at the University of California at Santa Barbara, where I worked, began whispering that there were other kinds of whales—really big ones—off the coast.

"I decided to go on a 1-day whale-watching trip. It turned out to be one of the most amazing days of my life. As the boat headed out to sea, the water was absolutely flat. We could see for at least 20 or 30 miles (30 or 50 kilometers) in every direction.

"When the boat was about 3 miles (5 km) from Santa Cruz Island, someone suddenly pointed to the

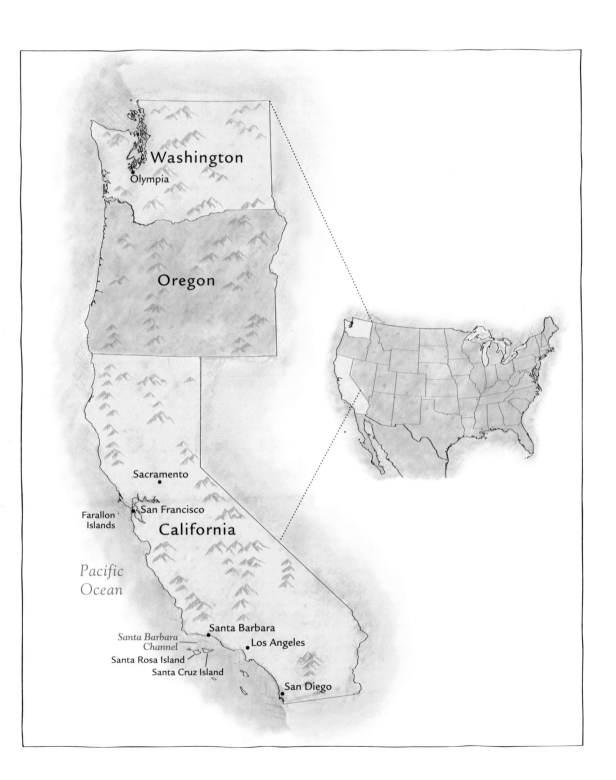

Washington

Olympia

Oregon

Sacramento

San Francisco

Farallon
Islands

California

Pacific
Ocean

Santa Barbara

Santa Barbara
Channel

Los Angeles

Santa Rosa Island

Santa Cruz Island

San Diego

south. About 2 or 3 miles (3 or 5 km) away, we saw the sun reflect off something large and shiny. It was the back of a blue whale! Before the day was done, we saw more than a half a dozen blue whales up close and personal. We also saw humpback whales, minke whales, hundreds of dolphins, porpoises, sea lions, and all kinds of other amazing marine life.

"That day left a deep impression on me. I began to wonder how many blue whales lived along the Pacific coast and what they were doing there. The captain of the whale-watching boat had talked about a

The author helps a young friend named Nathan Jess learn about whales.

man who was studying the whales. That man was John Calambokidis (KAL-am-BO-kee-dees).

"I called John, and he graciously shared what he'd learned. I wrote about what he told me in an article for *The Christian Science Monitor*. A couple of years later, I started thinking that his work would also make a fascinating book. Over the next few months, I interviewed John several more times and visited his office in Olympia, Washington.

"Most of the information in this book is based on those interviews and visits with John. I gathered additional information from various books and science articles. Many of these were written by John and his wife, Gretchen Steiger. I relied heavily on these sources because many books and articles about whales are out-of-date or incorrect.

"Writing this book has been exciting for me because I know that it contains new and surprising information about the largest animals on Earth."

On a clear day, the spout of a blue whale can be seen from several miles away.

Setting Out

A *summer morning dawns along the California coast.* The sun still hides behind the coastal mountains and fog sits like a wet blanket over the Pacific Ocean. Biologist John Calambokidis does a final check of his fuel, equipment, and supplies. Then he fires up the engine of his 18-foot (5.5-meter) inflatable boat and heads out to sea.

John isn't exactly sure where he's going, but he knows what he's looking for. Through the mist, he steers his craft 20 miles (32 km) across the Santa Barbara Channel. He passes the silent, rocky cliffs of Santa Cruz Island until he finds himself between the islands of Santa Cruz and Santa Rosa.

Suddenly, the fog burns off. The sunlight transforms the sea from leaden gray to dazzling blue. Then John sees a misty spray of water shooting up from the ocean surface. It's a spout—a whale spout.

The spout comes from a blue whale—the world's largest animal. There's not just one spout either. Scanning the sea around him, John counts five, six, seven spouts within 1 mile (1.6 km) of one another. He smiles. Even from a distance, he can hear the animals' great watery breaths. "Pshhh! Pshhh! Pshhh!" They sound like the heaving gasps of a steam locomotive.

John steers his boat cautiously among the giants. Each whale is more than 80 feet (24 m) long—almost five times longer than his boat. With a flick of its tail, any one of these giant creatures could easily smash John and his boat to bits. But John has learned that the whales won't hurt him. The whales are feeding. They are diving down 200 or 300 feet (61 or 91 m) to swallow huge schools of shrimp-like animals called krill.

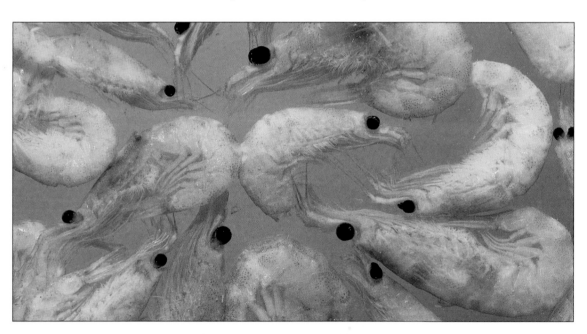

Krill are the main prey for blue whales and several other kinds of large whales.

The whales stay underwater for 5 minutes, sometimes longer. Then they surface, sending up 30-foot (9-m) spouts of watery spray as they let air out of automobile-size lungs and breathe in again.

John carefully writes down his location, the number of whales he sees, the time of day, and other information that may come in handy later. Then he picks up his camera and begins to photograph the ocean giants.

Biologist Beginnings

Unlike most whale watchers, John doesn't take pictures for fun. He is working. His job is to study the large whales off the Pacific coast. John's most important tool is a camera. He has been gathering information about whales with his camera since 1986, but his passion for marine mammals began long before that.

As a young boy, John loved nature and wondered how he could help protect it. After high school, he traveled to Africa and the Middle East. On this journey, he came face-to-face with hyenas, lions, and other large, wild animals. His interest in mammals began to grow.

John's interest in mammals began to develop when he saw African wildlife firsthand.

When he returned to the United States, John became a student at Evergreen State College in Olympia, Washington. There he learned that seals, whales, and other marine mammals in the nearby Pacific Ocean face many dangers. John wanted to help these animals.

In college, he designed a study to find out how pollution affects harbor seals. After he graduated in 1978, John and several other scientists started a non-profit group called Cascadia Research. They took the name from the nearby Cascade Mountains. The scientists' mission was to learn more about marine mammals and to find ways to protect them.

John discusses a research project with other scientists at Cascadia Research's main office in Olympia, Washington.

John's early work focused on smaller marine mammals such as harbor seals.

Following his passion wasn't easy. John soon discovered that even though most people are interested in whales and other marine mammals, it is hard to get money to study them. "In Washington State, there are probably hundreds of people working on fish compared to a few dozen who work on marine mammals," he explains. "Despite the popularity of marine mammals, it's a real struggle to find support for answering even basic questions about them."

To do their research, John and the team of scientists he works with apply for grants—money given to scientists by the National Science Foundation and other government agencies. The scientists at Cascadia Research used their first grants to study how pollution affects seals, harbor porpoises, and other small marine mammals that live in Puget Sound, Washington. Then, in 1986, John won a 3-year grant to study humpback whales at the Farallon Islands Marine Sanctuary in northern California.

This humpback whale is breaching.

Giant Surprises

People have long been fascinated by humpback whales. These whales are famous for their "songs"—the enchanting calls they use to communicate with one another. Humpbacks are also known for their acrobatics. They have been observed spy-hopping (sticking their heads straight up out of the water), breaching (leaping out of the water), and even playing with logs and other objects on the ocean surface.

Humpback Whales	
SCIENTIFIC NAME:	*Megaptera novaeangliae*
KIND OF WHALE:	Baleen whale
FOOD:	Krill, fish, small ocean animals
GREATEST LENGTH:	52 feet (15.8 m)
MAXIMUM SPEED:	10–12 nautical miles (18–22 km/hour)
LIFESPAN:	Unknown, possibly up to 100 years
LOCATION:	Worldwide
POPULATION:	Estimated at 10,000 to 15,000

Unfortunately, the humpback is one of several kinds of whales that has been hunted nearly to extinction. At the end of the 1800s, large whaling ships armed with exploding harpoons began to search the world's oceans for whales. They slaughtered hundreds of thousands of whales for their meat, oil, baleen, and other useful products.

The killing finally stopped in the 1960s, when people realized that humpbacks and other kinds of whales were nearly extinct. Since that time, biologists have been studying whales. They hope to find ways to increase the number of whales in the ocean.

In the early 1980s, scientists decided to study the humpbacks that spend part of the year near the Farallon Islands. John's job was to count the whales and to find out where they came from, what they were doing there, and where they went when they left the area. The information John and his team collected would be used to make decisions about protecting these whales.

The first large whales John studied were feeding around the Farallon Islands in northern California.

John began observing the whales from airplanes and sailboats. Almost immediately, he got a huge surprise. Some of the whales he saw were not humpbacks—they were blue whales.

Blue whales are the largest animals on Earth. They can grow up to 89 feet (27 m) long and weigh as much as 320,000 pounds (145,000 kilograms)!

A blue whale breaching close to shore

Blue whales usually feed alone or in pairs. Their favorite food is krill. A blue whale traps krill in the comb-like baleen plates in its mouth and slurps down the tiny animals with its giant tongue.

Most blue whales live far from shore, so very few scientists have studied them in the wild. When John discovered the blue whales off the coast of California, he knew it was a rare opportunity to learn more about Earth's largest animals. He decided to include the blue whales in his study.

When money for the project ran out in 1988, John applied for a new grant. Southwest Fisheries Science Center in La Jolla, California, gave Cascadia Research money to study whales along the coasts of California, Oregon, Washington, Mexico, and Central America.

Whale Matchmakers

A big part of John's job is to identify and observe the behaviors of individual whales. To identify a humpback, John photographs the underside of the whale's tail, or fluke. To identify a blue whale, he photographs

If you look closely at these two blue whales, you can see differences in the pigment patterns on their skin.

the dorsal fin—the fin at the back of its body—and pigment patterns on the whale's skin. These features are different in each whale and change little during a whale's lifetime, so they can be used for identification—just as fingerprints are used to identify people.

Over the years, John and the scientists who work with him have created a whale photo library that allows them to identify and recognize individual whales. Each time he goes out to sea, John takes photographs of the whales he finds. When the photos are developed, John compares them to the photos in the library. If a new photo matches an old one, John knows he's found a whale that he's seen before. If he doesn't find a match, he adds the photo of the "new" whale to the collection.

John's work is not as simple as it sounds. He often travels great distances to find and photograph

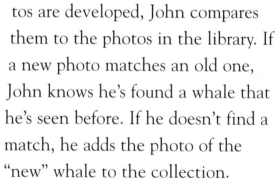

The photos that make up Cascadia Research's whale library are kept in three-ring binders. By comparing new photos to ones in the library, scientists can determine how many humpback and blue whales live off the Pacific Coast.

John and his biologist wife Gretchen often cover huge distances in their small inflatable boat.

whales. Sometimes he covers more than 220 miles (350 km) in a single day. Large waves can make it difficult to navigate his tiny boat. When the weather is bad, he often has trouble finding his way back to shore. In thick fog, John has come dangerously close to being run over by large oil tankers and other ships.

Over the years, however, John's dedication has paid off. He and his team have built up one of the largest photographic libraries of humpback and blue whales in the world.

Imagine you're John Calambokidis. Yesterday you went out in your boat and photographed the flukes of several humpback whales. You just picked up prints of your film. Do any of the new photos match ones you've seen before?

Compare the photograph above from yesterday's trip to the photo library on the right. Pay special attention to the coloration of the flukes, the scars, and the pattern along the top edge of each fluke. Can you find a match?

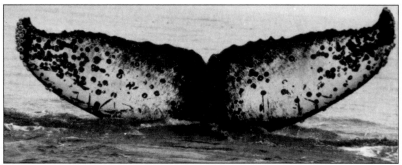

Chapter 3

Counting Whales

When John and his team started their work, one of their main goals was to estimate the number of whales off the coast of California. Scientists wanted to know whether these whale populations were increasing from year to year. The answer to this question would help scientists find ways to protect the whales.

John was the first person to estimate the size of California's blue and humpback whale populations.

Blue Whales	
SCIENTIFIC NAME:	*Balaenoptera musculus*
KIND OF WHALE:	Baleen whale
FOOD:	Krill, red crabs, smaller animals
GREATEST LENGTH:	98 feet (29.9 m), possibly longer
MAXIMUM SPEED:	20 nautical miles (37 km/hour)
LIFESPAN:	Unknown, possibly up to 100 years
LOCATION:	Worldwide
POPULATION:	Estimated at less than 5,000

To do this, he counted the total number of whales his team had identified since they began their study. Then he counted the number of new whales his team had identified during the past year. He plugged these numbers into a special mathematical formula and came up with an answer—910 humpback whales and 2,000 blue whales swim off the coast of California.

The number of blue whales surprised John and his team. As small as it was, the blue whale population they were studying was the largest anywhere on

John and his team were surprised to find out that one of the largest blue whale populations in the world lives off the Pacific Coast.

Earth. At one time, hundreds of thousands of blue whales swam in the world's oceans. But, like humpbacks, blue whales were almost wiped out by commercial whaling.

Between 1920 and 1970, whalers killed more than 300,000 of these magnificent mammals. The slaughter continued even after hunting blue whales became illegal in the 1960s. Today, scientists believe that there are only about 5,000 blue whales in the entire world.

So why are there so many off the coast of California?

"I think part of what's happened is that blue and humpback whales weren't hit as hard by whalers along the Californian and Mexican coasts as in other areas," says John. "It also looks like there [is now] more food off of California than in other areas. The whales are gathering where the food is."

An even more important question is: Are California's blue and humpback whale populations increasing? Are the whales recovering from the damage done by the whaling industry?

"One problem with making estimates is that no one really knows how many whales were left when whaling stopped," explains John. "Many estimates

A female humpback whale and her calf

came from the whalers themselves. These [estimates] were based on how many whales they killed and the numbers were probably very unreliable.

"In 1998, we were able to determine for the first time that California's humpbacks are increasing at a rate of 6 to 8 percent each year. Because so many of California's blue whales still have to be identified, we don't know if their numbers are also increasing. It will probably take us several more years to find that out."

A researcher at Cascadia Research adds a new photo to the whale library. Scientists can use the library to track whales.

Tracking Giants

Cascadia's photo library can be used for more than just counting whales. The library makes it possible for John and his team to track these giant creatures. As a result, the scientists can now determine where and how the whales spend their time. This information adds to our basic knowledge of whale biology and behavior. It also helps scientists identify places that are important to whales.

Most large whales spend the summer and autumn feeding in higher latitudes, away from the equator. John's research has confirmed that California's humpback and blue whales spend their summers following schools of krill up and down the coasts of California, Oregon, and Washington. For example, the whales John originally observed near the Farallon Islands were there to feed on krill.

However, before John began his research project, no one knew where California's humpback and blue whales spent the winter. To find out, John has spent

From this sailboat, John has photographed whales off the coast of Mexico and Central America during the winter.

the last several winters photographing whales in Mexico and Central America. He has also been gathering whale photographs from scientists working in other parts of the Pacific Ocean. This work has revealed some surprising information.

John and his team have discovered that many of California's humpbacks spend time off the coast of Baja California and mainland Mexico during the winter. Others have turned up in Costa Rica. Three California humpbacks have even been "matched" to whales that winter near Hawaii!

California's humpback whales spend their winters off the coast of Mexico, Costa Rica, and Hawaii.

This blue whale is lunge-feeding.

John has also learned where California's blue whales spend the winter. In January and March 1999, he searched for blue whales off the coast of Central America. In an area called the Costa Rica Dome, he

photographed thirteen blue whales. More than half of them were from California. Based on these sightings, John believes that a large number of California's blue whales spend the winter off the coast of Costa Rica.

Blue Whale Feeding Frenzy

In his searches for whales, John has had some unforgettable adventures. Not long ago, John and his wife, fellow biologist Gretchen Steiger, spent several weeks searching for whales off the coast of Baja California. One evening, they suddenly found themselves surrounded by forty blue whales. The whales were feeding on enormous schools of tiny red crabs close to the ocean surface. Many of the whales were lunge-feeding—making fast, sideways swipes at the crabs. Other whales were attacking the crabs from below.

"We were leaning over the side of the boat, looking through the clear water at what seemed to be millions

During one amazing encounter, John and Gretchen watched blue whales feeding on a school of small red crabs off the coast of Baja California.

of crabs as deep as we could see," John recalls. "Suddenly, all the crabs opened up their pincers in a threatened pose and the huge, open jaws of a blue whale rose from the depths. The whale swallowed the tiny creatures and then disappeared again.

"We realized with alarm that our small inflatable boat would easily fit into a whale's mouth, but in the middle of this incredible feeding process, it was really hard to leave. We ended up spending four more glorious days with this group of blue whales. We were able to get good identification shots and witness more of their amazing feeding behavior."

The Oldest Whale

No one knows for sure how long large whales live, but Cascadia's photo library has provided some interesting clues. As Richard Sears, one of the scientists who works with John, flipped through a guidebook, he came across a photo of a blue whale that he had taken 25 years ago.

Amazingly, John's team had recent photos of the same whale in its library—proof that blue whales can live at least 25 years. John has "matched" several other whales to photographs taken more than 20 years ago. As John's work continues, he will learn more about how long whales live.

This humpback whale is lunge-feeding.

Life Among the Whales

The whales off the coast of California provide a special opportunity for many scientists to answer questions about the ocean's giants. In addition to their own work, John and his team are currently investigating whale feeding habits, the relationships between whales, and the birth and death rates of large whales.

When he's not out photographing whales, John spends his time writing reports, analyzing data, and raising money to keep Cascadia Research going. His work is challenging and requires long hours. Sometimes, he has little time to spend with his wife and their two children, Alexei and Zoe.

So why does he keep doing it? "There are a number of things I really love about doing this work," John says. "I love being out on the water, and not just because of the whales. There's also the real challenge of dealing with ocean conditions that can be very physically demanding. Sometimes I'm out there for more than 15 hours at a time. I know that if anything goes wrong, I can be in serious trouble."

The sight of a blue whale surfacing is unforgettable—even to someone who has seen it many times before.

What about being with the whales?

"I've spent time with thousands of whales," John says. "But to me, the sight and sound of a blue whale surfacing in the sea is still breathtaking. Even after spending the last 12 years studying them, I have experiences with these animals that amaze me."

One such experience, John explains, is the appearance of "friendly whales." When John began his research, whales avoided contact with his boat. Then in 1992, one or two humpback whales approached

John's boat and began pushing it around. This frightened John at first, but the whales didn't seem to want to hurt him. One whale pushed the boat in a circle with its pectoral fins. Another whale actually lifted the boat several feet out of the water on its back.

Since 1992, the number of friendly whale incidents has increased each year. This is just one of the reasons that John continues to be fascinated by whales.

Ballerinas of the Sea

John is impressed by a whale's ability to control its enormous body. "These whales have a degree of bodily control that is literally unimaginable for their size," he says. "I've had animals spy-hop right next to my boat. I reach out to touch them and when my hand gets a few inches from their heads, they lean back just an inch or two to keep away from my hand. Of course, many times a whale lets me touch its head, but you can feel the level of control. They are extremely tactile animals, too. They are very aware of any touch."

Whales in Danger

Every year, many whales drown in fishing nets. Collisions with boats kill others. Pollution may also be harming these ocean giants. Knowing the number and habits of whales helps scientists understand how these dangers affect entire whale populations. That is one reason why John's research is so important.

Whales also face a more direct threat. Although whaling has been banned, several countries—including Norway, Japan, and Russia—want to begin hunting whales again. In fact, Norway and Japan have been illegally hunting minke whales for the past few years. As a biologist, John opposes commercial whaling.

This minke whale is diving to look for food.

Many people go on whale watching tours each year. The amount of money tourists pay for these trips is greater than the amount that could be earned from commercial whaling.

"There are a number of reasons why whales are poor choices for hunting," he explains. "They reproduce very slowly and are slow to recover from hunting." A female blue whale can't reproduce until she is about 5 years old. Even then, she will have only one baby every 2 years.

"Whales are also extremely hard to study, so it's difficult to make sure we're not overhunting them," adds John. He points out that commercial whale-watching boats bring in far more money from tourists than killing whales would bring. Because of their size and beauty, many people find whales fascinating. They help us understand our connection to the other living things on Earth.

"I would never want to see the extinction of any kind of whale," says John. "I would never want to deny future generations from appreciating and enjoying these huge animals." John and his co-workers plan to continue their whale research as long as they can find the money to do it.

Following Your Dreams

Would you like to study whales too? You can begin by doing well in school. Then you can study marine biology and animal behavior in college. You can start now by reading other books about whales. If you live near the ocean, find out if scientists at a local aquarium or marine park are studying whales.

Most of all, it is important to remember that living your dreams takes dedication. Many people want to study whales, but very few jobs are available. John encourages students who are interested in whales and other marine mammals to follow their hearts.

"Find the things you love to do and enjoy doing," he says. "Then, really pursue them. Even if it's challenging, you can find a way to do it."

To be a marine biologist, you need dedication, good study habits, and plenty of heart. These scientists are trying to save some whales that have beached themselves.

John knows what he's talking about. He is living proof that following your heart will lead you to the ocean of your dreams.

Important Words

krill   (noun) a small shrimplike animal

lunge-feed   (verb) a marine mammal's fast, sideways swipes at its prey, usually at the ocean surface

mammal   (noun) a warm-blooded animal that has a backbone and feeds its young with mother's milk

population   (noun) the total number of individuals of a species living in an area

prey   (noun) an animal that is hunted and eaten by another animal

spy-hop   (verb) a marine mammal behavior that involves sticking its head straight up out of the water

tactile   (adjective) having to do with the sense of touch

To Find Out More

Books   Hundreds of books have been published about whales and whaling. A few of my favorites are listed below.

Calambokidis, John and Gretchen Steiger. *Blue Whales.* Stillwater, MN: Voyageur Press, 1997.

Ellis, Richard. *Men and Whales.* New York: Knopf, 1991.

Gowell, Elizabeth Tayntor. *Whales and Dolphins: What They Have in Common.* Danbury, CT: Franklin Watts, 2000.

Kraus, Scott. *The Search for the Right Whale.* New York: Crown, 1993.

Murphy, Jim. *Gone A-Whaling.* New York: Clarion Books, 1998.

Patent, Dorothy Hinshaw. *Whales: Giants of the Deep.* New York: Holiday House, 1984.

Pringle, Laurence. *Dolphin Man.* New York: Atheneum, 1995.

Organizations and Online Sites

Cascadia Research

http://www.CascadiaResearch.org/

This site lists the most recent results of the work of John Calambokidis and other scientists. Find out about the Adopt-a-Whale project that is co-sponsored by Cascadia Research and the Oceanic Society.

The Center for Whale Studies Multi-Media Library

http://www.cfws.org/gallery/whale2.jpg

At this site, you'll find photos of all sorts of whales.

International Whaling Commission

http://ourworld.compuserve.com/homepages/iwcoffice

This site has up-to-date information on international decisions and events that affect whales and whaling.

The Oceanic Society

Fort Mason Center, Building E
San Francisco, CA 94123

WhaleNet

http://whale.wheelock.edu/

This site has links to all kinds of sites with information about whale research. Check out the section specifically designed for students.

Whale Songs

http://whales.ot.com/

Follow the experiences of an American science teacher who spent a week onboard *Song of the Whale*, a research vessel used to study whales and other ocean animals.

Wildlife Conservation Society

http://www.wcs.org

2300 Southern Blvd.

Bronx, NY 10460-1099

Index

Photographs ©: Animals Animals: 11 (A. & M. Shah), 34 (Lewis S. Trusty); Cascadia Research: 22, 23 top, 23 center right, 23 center left (John Calambokidis), 23 bottom (Joseph Evenson); Liaison Agency, Inc.: 43 (Stephen Rose); Mark J. Rauzon: 32, 33; Peter Arnold Inc.: 36, 38 (Mark Carwardine/Still Pictures), 39 (Doug Perrine); Photo Researchers: 40 (Ray Gilbert), 19, 25, 41 (Francois Gohier), 18, 31 (Bud Lehnhausen), 10 (Tom McHugh), border art, back cover, 1 (G. Carleton Ray), 16, 17 (William E. Townsend Jr.); Sneed B. Collard III: 21 (John Cubbage), 6 (M. Mortezalefari), 4, 12, 20, 28, 30; Tony Stone Images: cover (Kim Heacox), 27 (Darryl Torckler), 14 (Stuart Westmorland); Visuals Unlimited: 8 (Daniel W. Gotshall), 13 (Len Rue Jr.).